T0196382

THE BAY OF THE
MOTHER OF GOD

THE BAY OF THE MOTHER OF GOD

A Yankee Discovers the Chesapeake Bay

George R. Merrill

authorHOUSE®

AuthorHouse™
1663 Liberty Drive
Bloomington, IN 47403
www.authorhouse.com
Phone: 1-800-839-8640

© 2013 by George R. Merrill. All rights reserved.

No part of this book may be reproduced, stored in a retrieval system, or transmitted by any means without the written permission of the author.

Published by AuthorHouse   05/28/2013

ISBN: 978-1-4817-5631-0 (sc)
ISBN: 978-1-4817-5630-3 (e)

Library of Congress Control Number: 2013909509

Any people depicted in stock imagery provided by Thinkstock are models, and such images are being used for illustrative purposes only.
Certain stock imagery © Thinkstock.

This book is printed on acid-free paper.

Because of the dynamic nature of the Internet, any web addresses or links contained in this book may have changed since publication and may no longer be valid. The views expressed in this work are solely those of the author and do not necessarily reflect the views of the publisher, and the publisher hereby disclaims any responsibility for them.

CONTENTS

PEOPLE AND PLACES

THE TERRAIN

CRITTERS

FLORA

SAILING INTO THE SUNSET

DEDICATION

To Jo, with whom I shared the wonders of the Chesapeake Bay and
who patiently rescued me from the snares of cyberspace.

ACKNOWLEDGMENTS

Thanks to Wilson W. Wyatt Jr., editor of *The Delmarva Review,* for his continuing support of my writing, and to Jeanne Pinault, who takes commas very seriously. I owe an abiding debt to Annie Dillard and Lewis Thomas, whose writings first introduced me to the pure pleasure of reading and writing the essay.

I want to thank two other writers who offered encouraging comments about some earlier essays of mine: author and actor Ben Stein, who wrote that I was a "born poet," and Marian Fontana *(Widows Walk: A Memoir of 9/11),* who generously raised comparisons to Whitman and Thoreau. Their words have buoyed me up immeasurably, and I hope the current work does not let them—or any other readers—down

Fairlee Creek

THE BAY OF THE
MOTHER OF GOD

I arrived in Baltimore in 1973 via New York City and Connecticut, where I'd lived most of my life. In 1974, when I sailed from Middle River on the Western Shore of the Bay to Fairlee Creek, my first port of call on the Eastern Shore, I discovered the Chesapeake Bay.

In 1570, a lone Spanish vessel sailed into the Chesapeake Bay. The Spanish, perhaps the first Europeans to have seen it, named the Bay *Bahia de Madre de Dios*, or the Bay of the Mother of God.

That name, Bay of the Mother of God, suggests to me that what they saw and experienced on their arrival held spiritual significance for them. Brother Carrera, a religious sailing with the Spanish expedition wrote of the Bay that it was "a great and beautiful port . . . in it there are many deep water ports, each better than the next." As the Blessed Mother Mary of Catholicism had been to the Spanish faithful, the Bay, too, may have also felt welcoming and hospitable while offering refuge and safety to the travelers.

The following are essays accompanied by my photographs. They describe some of the discoveries I made living and sailing around the Chesapeake Bay. The stories are true, many are playful, and all are reflective. My discoveries in themselves were unremarkable.

However, I felt as I lived them out that they had a spiritual character to them, the kind that assumes that the total of an experience equals more than the sum of its parts.

My discoveries around the Bay were "each better than the next."

PEOPLE
AND
PLACES

Otis Turner

THE RIGHT TIME

Worship at nine, the sign read. My wife, Jo, and I arrived five minutes early. People stood around talking outside. At nine someone came with a key, opened the church, and let us file in. We were there that day to accompany my young mentee, Josh, because his grandmother couldn't be there with him. She worked weekends at a local motel. The church was St. Luke United Methodist Church, an old African American congregation in the small village of Bellevue, located on the Tred Avon River (a tributary of the Choptank River, which flows into the Chesapeake Bay). We belong to the small Episcopal Cathedral in nearby Easton. Our church has no black parishioners.

Well after nine, everyone was in the church still talking, milling about, hugging and shaking hands. It didn't seem worship would begin any time soon.

Josh is ten years old, an African American. We're a good match. We like each other. We meet to play dominoes, ride bikes, carve pumpkins at Halloween, play catch, and take dinghy rides on the River, "He has a smile that would melt stone," his teacher told me once. She's right.

Josh lives with his grandmother and grandfather. His grandmother, Lillie Mae, gets on his case when he doesn't do his schoolwork and she clearly loves him to death She works hard at the motel to make ends meet. Both of Josh's grandparents have health problems. His grandfather, Robert watches television and smokes cigarettes most of the day. He can't quit. It worries Lillie Mae; when she comes home from shopping she tells him she forgot the cigarettes he'd asked her to get or that they were out of them. Robert drives Josh to school events and takes Lillie Mae back and forth to work. He's a steady man.

They live in a house built by Habitat for Humanity that brought them from their house in Cordova to Bellevue. The old house was in disrepair and out in the country. It was difficult for them to move. The family had a long history in Cordova. Lillie Mae and Josh were active in the church nearby, but the move precluded them continuing. Jo and I offered to get Josh started in church until Lillie Mae's schedule would allow her to begin attending. She welcomed the idea.

We settled in a pew just behind Otis Turner, a lifelong church member whom I'd met three years prior. He told me that he never once missed church. Otis quit working the Chesapeake Bay, where he'd spent his life oystering, crabbing, and skippering packets carrying produce from the Shore to Baltimore. He was then over ninety. Now he goes down to the workboats along the river to talk to waterman. He holds forth like a revivalist preacher, reverently invoking the Lord's name, while reviewing with anyone who will listen the history of his own salvation. His nephew told me, "He'll talk your ears till they fall off." Otis wearies neither of well doing nor of talking.

I spent a morning sitting with him near the water, by an old workboat called the *Amen*.

"Had no drop of liquor since I was sixteen. Got bad drunk once, but I asked the Lord to take the taste away. He did. Ain't had no drink since." He told me that he had buried three wives and had lived alone for many years. "No woman has ever crossed my doorstep since my wives passed," he'd say and shake his head pensively. Some people have lectured me on their morality, and I'll feel as if I'm being bludgeoned. Otis's moral reveries seemed different, as if he were telling me fondly about the precious moments of his life, the holy hours. His eyes, already beginning to cloud with age, reveal the pleasure he feels in his recollections. I think these stories represent the times he's had with God—he'll tell you that.

Otis has a theory about the calamitous reduction of the oyster and crab population in the Bay. "Ain't Dermo or the MSX virus, it's sin doin' it. We ain't treatin' the Bay right," he'd look at me earnestly.

"It's 'cause people follow the devil and they think it's alright. You see, folks think the Devil is red with a pitchfork, steamin' from the fires of hell, ugly as sin." He laughs, "No way, he looks as pretty as you please so folks get fooled into thinking what he's tellin' them is good. We ain't treatin' the Bay right, but the Devil says don't pay that talk no mind."

Geese fly over, making a ruckus so I can barely hear him; he pauses for a moment to watch them go by. "Folks get fooled into thinkin' what's good is bad, and what's bad is good. Now tell me that ain't so." I allow as to how it is so.

I once came by to give him a photograph I had taken of him by the workboat called *Amen*. At home, Otis was sitting in an old stuffed chair, a frayed Bible next to him. Three young women happened to come to the door, Jehovah's Witnesses. One was in charge, the other two interns. Otis was an easy mark for their evangelistic practice, since he would be one of the few who would always invite them in.

Their task was clear: manoeuver Otis into saying the word "Jehovah" each time the word "Lord" arose in the conversation. "The Lord only do I serve," he insisted. The Jehovah's Witnesses pressed their case hard, but Otis stuck to his "Lord." The thrust and parry of semantics finally became a polite verbal power struggle, religious discussions, as they're called. I prayed to the "Lord" for Otis's total victory over the warriors of Jehovah. He never once said the word *Jehovah*.

It was sad that these good people couldn't hear the spiritual music of Otis's life for the dogmatic imperatives they invested in their own words. They left. Otis confided that they had been there before. "They vex my spirit," he said, wagging his head wearily.

I introduced Josh to Otis at church, saying that Otis was the oldest man in Bellevue. Otis looked at Josh and then me and said, "Instruct them in their youth, and they will walk in the way," slightly raising his index finger, and, as if to further the weight of his authority, added, "Proverbs."

By now it was nine thirty-five. A choir of about ten began singing while marching down the aisle from the back of the church to the sanctuary, swaying rhythmically from side to side to the steady cadence of the music, repeating the words, "Oh, how I love Jesus." The music, warm and somnambulistic, mesmerized me the way monks do when chanting plainsong.

There was no preacher. Lay leadership took the service. All was not smooth. The lay leader couldn't pronounce the word *apostolic*.

One or two people said it for her and she moved on. Once the organist began playing a hymn, but not the one the choir was singing. He stopped and they started again. No one seemed to mind.

A man offered the prayer for the community and its people. He was short, seemingly at least ten years older than Otis, and bent almost in half. He negotiated the route from the choir to the chancel tentatively. Would he fall? No one seemed concerned, as if they were sure that in good time he would get where he needed to. He did, rendering his prayer clearly, spontaneously, on bended knee from which I was sure he would never rise. He concluded and made his way back. The service was guided by a grace that everyone took for granted was present. It was as though the community of this people, not the performance of liturgy, was what this time was about—take care of one another and God would take care of the rest.

In the preacher's absence, the choir offered a "Sermon in Song." The music was bouncy; the congregation became increasingly festive with each song. At the hymn's end, shouts of "Amen" and "Yeah" went up. Then the choir launched into another.

Josh folded his bulletin to make paper airplanes. He'd grow sleepy at times. I touched his shoulder to the rhythm of the music. He'd smile. My wife finds sermons tedious, but she loves music. When we learned that there wasn't going to be a sermon, she said, "God is good."

The moment had caught me up and tears came to my eyes. Why? Everyone was happy. Perhaps it was because I'm an Episcopalian. For me, betraying my emotions in public is bad form, but I was strongly moved by the spirit that hovered over the community.

The lay leader asked for prayers and special concerns. Someone approached her. The lay leader laid hands on her. They spoke, I couldn't hear. They stood close, touching, and finally disengaged, the woman returned to her place. The lay leader went back to the podium. She wiped tears from her eyes. Then, in what seemed like sun coming out from behind a rain cloud, she stood with her face smiling and radiant and said, "The Lord has blessed me." The congregation nodded and said, "Yeah."

We passed the peace: People sought us out extending us a hearty welcome. I moved from one person to another, like stepping the "grand right and left" in a square dance, where one person lets you go while another takes your hand so someone is always reaching out to you.

One elderly woman sat at the end of the pew and she seemed unable to get to the aisle. I reached out my hand to her to exchange the peace. She sat there impassively, staring right past me. A man behind me, addressing me as "brother," said gently in a matter-of-fact way, "Sister Dora is blind." I felt foolish. Without thinking I asked the man if he thought it would be all right if I just took her hand. "She'd like that right much," he assured me. I did and she took mine in both of hers. Her face rose to mine and I saw in her sightless eyes what I thought was compassion.

"Where are we?" Josh inquired as he dismantled his last airplane.

"Offertory," I said.

"What's that?"

"That's when they take the money."

"I didn't bring money." he replied.

"We'll use mine."

"When's church over?"

"When it's time."

He looked at me smiling as if he thought I was teasing him.

After the choir marched down the aisle singing "Oh, how I love Jesus." the service ended. No one was in a hurry to leave. Josh met a little girl he knew. She didn't want to let him go. The girl's mother said, "I got to be keeping my eye on you, fussin' with boys like that."

Josh grew tired of his temptress and started walking home.

"Want to go again, sometime?" I asked him.

"Yeah, I guess."

Otis was walking to his home nearby. I drove past him and waved. I'm not sure he knew me. It was his eyes; they looked as if they were filled with tears, but I don't think they were tears; his eyes were full of years, the years of life in the church in Bellevue and on the Chesapeake Bay, the Bay of the Mother of God. Otis told me once he was waiting for his Lord to call him home. "When it's time, I'll be ready to go," he mused.

The sign said the service began at nine, and at first I thought the "service" started late. Now I think it began the moment the first person arrived. Clocks tell time accurately, but they can never tell us the right time. Only a community of people who care for each other will know just what that right time is.

Significant Other

A SHOW OF HANDS

Driving through St. Michaels in the summer, I see tourists everywhere, like ants at a picnic. They cover the sidewalks like flowing lava, spilling over into the street, crossing in undesignated areas, grinding traffic to a halt. As a resident, I groused to my wife one day about our weekly invasion of aliens. Jo remarked, "It's sweet to see people holding hands."

I'd never noticed. Wherever I looked I saw people holding hands. My eyes were opened and I saw our town differently. I'd assumed that only young lovers held hands in public. Not so here. Couples well up in years, their silvery heads glistening in the midday sun, shopping bags in tow, were walking hand in hand. They enjoyed being in St. Michaels and being with each other. I saw spouses, children and parents, and a gay couple all holding hands.

Regarding tourists, I'm now a kinder and gentler man. On weekends, I look for this tender expression of affection and on a quick drive by one day I counted no less than fifteen couples handholding.

I used to regard tourists as a subspecies of the vulture. They descended in droves, landing where the sale items stood for the picking. They'd crowd the landscape, forage for a day or so, and then return to their nests far away, leaving behind them the effluence of their presence—water bottles, paper cups, plates, plastic bags, promotional flyers, and newspapers floating in the wind. On Mondays, the parking spots at the Acme, occupied only the day before by herds of SUVs, were now liberated and available again to residents.

If St. Michaels can encourage such affectionate demonstrations, I say "so what" if I must park a half a mile from the Acme to get milk or wait a few minutes for a family to cross the street in undesignated areas.

Sadly, the word "touching" has earned a sinister connotation these days. We need touch to survive just as we need touch to nurture mutual affection. Monkeys know this, and after a fight they hold hands as a sign of reconciliation. Holding hands immediately comforts children and in hospitals, as soon as the nurse touches her patient, blood pressure drops and the patient feels safe.

Science is studying the act of handholding. Tiffany Field, director of the Touch Research Institute at the University of Miami, observes, "Based on what we've seen, when we get more physical intimacy, we get better relationships." Stephanie Rosenbloom, writing for the *New York Times,* has investigated handholding among college students and says: "There seemed to be two universal truths: that handholding is the least nauseating public display of affection and has become more significant than other seemingly deeper expressions of love and romance." One student allowed, "It's a lot more intimate to hold hands nowadays than to kiss."

Holding hands requires certain skills. In the case of my wife and me it means, literally, managing the long and short of it. Jo has longer legs than I have and stands a hair taller. I have a long torso and short legs. Our hands do not meet naturally as they hang at our sides. To further complicate the matter, she prefers holding hands with her knuckles facing forward. So do I. To make the handholding a mutually satisfying experience requires a trade-off. I will take Jo's hand the way I prefer, and shortly afterward defer to her preferences. It helps to regulate our differences by conscious choices. Regulating differences is one of human kind's greatest challenges. Our survival depends on regulating differences, and marriages can't live without it.

In today's troubled world, the Eastern Shore's St. Michaels deserves a show of hands for inspiring expressions of affection in its visitors. And yes, for also inspiring kindness in one of its grouchier, but now more enlightened, residents.

Truckin'

KEEP ON TRUCKIN'

On the Eastern Shore of Maryland, pickup trucks are as numerous as geese and mosquitoes. Many are the kind I remember as a kid: built to haul and carry the stuff of a workingman's trade and the fruits of his labor. Such trucks were a no-frills, no-nonsense tool in the service of getting one's job done, usually jobs that created a good deal of mess. The pickup truck was a guy thing.

Banged up and chipped, trucks I see here are mud-encrusted and rusting out. The cabs look as if they were never cleaned: cigarette butts litter the floor and, from an ashtray that has never been emptied, ashes pile high. Pop bottles and fast-food wrappers are scattered across the seats and floor like streets after a ticker-tape parade, and the haze on the inside of the windows, like cataracts on the eyes, makes the world seen from inside the cab appear soft and milky.

Mufflers hang tenuously with jury-rigged wires. I've seen their beds stacked so high that I was sure that when the driver accelerated his load would fall on the road. It rarely happens; the drivers are as skillful at the wheel as any jockey on his horse. However disreputable the pickup truck might appear, it gets you there, it's dependable, you can count on it.

Dogs are frequent passengers. They sit next to the driver, like a girlfriend or spouse. Women typically ride close to the male driver even if he's brought his dog along; in that case, although not always, the dog may be put in the rear bed. There, the dogs pace furiously back and forth in it as if the bed were a run: I'm always afraid that they'll fall out or jump off. Occasionally some do and are killed.

In perhaps more than half of the trucks, there's a gun rack in the cab that carries rifles, usually shotguns, but some carry bows, fishing rods, or just a hard hat on one prong. On trucks with guns in the gun rack, you may see bumper stickers expressing concern about gun control: "Fight the Gun Ban," reads a popular sticker. Others declare their passion for firearms more boldly, in stickers that read "Guns, Guts and Glory," the sentiment printed over the picture of a flowing stars and stripes. A carpenter's level is an occasional sight on gun racks, as if some truckers had beaten their swords into ploughshares.

Even though drivers are native to the area and know every inch of it, many drive slowly, looking around, savoring the passing landscape like tourists here for the first time. As you walk along the road, truck drivers with a hand on the wheel will raise the index finger of the same hand in an understated salutation, something I find remarkably friendly since the driver may be a total stranger to me.

Owners may name their trucks like we name pets. I've seen trucks called "Goosebuster," and "Sluefoot," and "Terminator"—names distinctly male, unlike the work boats here, which almost always bear women's names on their transoms. I saw one workboat called "Miss Behaving."

A genus may have varying species and a new kind of pickup truck has begun to appear on the Shore. They are smaller than the big Fords, Dodges, and GMCs and each one is squeaky clean—like my Uncle John's 1941 Chrysler that he washed weekly and dusted in between. A lot of them are Japanese models. The beds are like an old-fashioned parlor, cleaned for show but rarely used. You might eat off the floor of these cabs; they're immaculate. The drivers are men, too, but a different breed; they are commuters. Instead of plaid shirts and peaked caps with the name of feed companies and heavy machinery manufacturers on the crowns, the drivers wear banker's gray suits or blue blazers and rep ties from Brooks Brothers. They're not going to any dump or construction site but to law offices, public relations firms, brokerage houses, and government jobs across the Bridge in Washington or Baltimore. Instead of country music, their tape decks play Vivaldi or Mozart and their radios stay tuned for the latest on the stock market. The windows of the cabs are so clean they're invisible. And unlike their country cousins, who take each ride slowly, commuters drive their trucks at a furious clip as if they were not enjoying their time but are being driven by it, driven to get there, driven to get back.

I've wondered why such men would want to drive a pick up truck.

Maybe men in corporate America these days are feeling increasingly helpless by downsizing and competition, competing not with other men but with the power of some unseen electronic device that deletes a hundred jobs with the flick of a switch. The truck is one of those symbols of what "real men" once were: men who had control of their lives, who could choose to leave home, "go west" on the Conestoga wagon because there was something for them "out there." These men were, as trucks today are often advertised, rugged and tough. They got the job done and knew the value of a hard day's work. These were men at home in the outdoors who lived close to nature—in a word, men who felt confident of the world in which they lived.

I don't think men feel that way so much any more, and the pickup truck, as it takes us somewhere physically, may perhaps transport some of us psychologically to a time in which we felt close to the earth and more in control of our destinies.

God Love You

MEDITATION ON A SEPTIC TANK

On the rural landscape of the Shore we still occasionally see an outhouse. Septic tanks are more common, and we have one in our yard. On New Year's Day a few years ago, sewage began backing up into the shower. The septic service people responded immediately to our call for help and went about performing what most would consider an exceedingly unpleasant task. I went to speak to the technician as he was performing his ablutionary duties. He was bearded, young, handsome, and irrepressibly good-natured. He was very chatty. "This is really tough work, isn't it?" I ventured, by way of thanking him for responding so quickly. "We do it all the time," the technician told me, smiling, shrugging his shoulders philosophically, while placing a large hose down into our open septic tank to rid us of our waste.

In the mail the other day I received a card from the same septic service requesting that customers compose a "brief and inoffensive slogan," suitable for the sides of their trucks that carry the waste. The winner could receive one hundred dollars or equivalent septic services. I found the request challenging and mentioned it to my wife, along with a couple of ideas for slogans that had immediately sprang to mind. "Brief and inoffensive," she observed.

This kind of task, that of finding a helpful way of putting into words important things that might be delicate, disagreeable, even repulsive, is a crucial part of social life. Gracious words and the exercise of tact, which serve as humanity's most effective social lubricants, I fear don't grease the wheels of our daily conduct much any more, either in stores, on the street, or in the media. As a result, our cultural bearings are not only squeaking but are threatening to overheat and seize. The lack of graciousness in interpersonal situations can really back up on us and clog things up.

Recently, in the normal run of errands, I took notice of how many clerks in shops and stores extended me the normal courtesies of a greeting or even thanking me for my patronage. On good days, it was about eighty percent and on bad ones, about forty percent. On good days, the parting words were invariably, "Have a good one." Bad days included things like a clerk handing me change and not even making eye contact, looking put upon when asked for clarification, or responding to a question about merchandise by saying "I don't know" and not initiating some effort to get me the information. Even in the hallowed halls of many churches, newcomers complain that no one even takes the time to say hello.

In the entertainment arena, the four-letter word is more common than the use of the word *like* in the routine parlance of adolescents. ("It was, like, awesome!") And four-letter words, originally the staple of sub cultures, are now the daily fare of our social and so-called entertainment world, these words often issuing from the mouths of babes. The words arrest attention, but tell me nothing. There's a good reason for this.

Frequent use of expletives is not designed to communicate anything of substance but to obscure the relevant issue by creating an atmosphere of titillation. Psychotherapists caught on to that long ago. You're led to think, when hearing outrageous words, that you're hearing it "like it is," but on more sober reflection, the person is cloaking his or her actual feelings by using shocking or forbidden words—a little like a killdeer who fusses at you in order to draw your attention away from what he's really concerned about. To communicate, "like it is," for any of us, requires hard thinking and some knowledge and care in the use of words and some knowledge and care of the self. I suppose, in the absence of both an ability to think and to speak one's mind, a lot of four—letter words might at least fill the inner emptiness or turmoil they suggest and can provide temporary relief. Shakespeare said it as well as anybody: Tales told by idiots "are full of sound and fury, signifying nothing." Some who are not idiots, but hurt badly inside and don't know how to express it, may speak with sound and fury.

Most of my professional life was spent as a psychotherapist and priest. I worked with people for whom it was important to articulate critical experiences of their lives in order to heal. Often shame or pain-ridden, these people felt words would only condemn them further. They needed help in framing what they'd been through in words that would tell the truth but would not consign them to the cruel judgments of their own self-deprecation. This is also true of persons facing serious illnesses and other humiliations that life's circumstances impose; it's important to be able to speak the truth in ways that help us and others carry our burdens graciously. Such a task is hard work, and the tools we use are the care we take to find the right words.

Septic service personnel, like garbage men, aren't afforded the meritorious public recognition given, for example, to clergy, bank officers or military personnel. Septic and sanitation workers perform critical functions, not only for our health, but also for our self-esteem and sense of personal dignity. This is why I was pleased that my septic service offered the community an opportunity to do some hard thinking about how, in thought and word, we regard those who graciously perform for us life's less agreeable tasks. I did not submit a slogan, but I saw on one of their trucks the one they selected: "We like regular customers."

I confess that when the technician was working on our septic tank and preparing to take away the untended mess we'd created, I thought of God. It wasn't just that the beard he wore made him look a little like the image of Jesus that frequently appeared (before the advent of air conditioning) on the fans funeral homes issued to patrons. I was moved by how the technician handled the whole mess. Whenever I've created a distasteful situation in my life or in the lives of others and God seems to have intervened to help me clean it up, I've imagined God like the technician, going about the unpleasant task of helping me get it right, smiling kindly and saying, "I do it all time."

Door

DOORS ON THE SHORE

I'm routinely in and out of all sorts of things, but none more than doors.

Doors are a signature feature of my daily life. There's one at every turn. I would reckon that in the course of my lifetime, I've come and gone through millions of doors. Yet I never take notice of them. For something as omnipresent as they are, doors remain surprisingly invisible. And so, in reflection, I was surprised the other day that while driving, I noticed several doors. It wasn't as though I had to pass through any of them. I simply found the sight of them compelling, enough so that I pulled my car over to take a closer look. The doors were hanging in an old derelict motel located just north of Easton on Route 50. At first glance, the doors were a sorry sight.

The motel, the one-story kind, was set like row houses and arranged in a semi-circle forming a courtyard with a cement apron in front. There was rubble in the courtyard and hardly a pane of glass remained in any of the window frames. Inside the units I saw various castoffs: old furniture here, some wire there, metal cabinets there, a small stove. A couple of plastic chairs and a mattress in one unit suggested that maybe the motel still provided a modicum of hospitality to some less fortunate souls on their journey to and fro here on the Shore. My eyes were drawn again and again to the doors, most of them still intact, half open, their weathered fronts lit by the sun, highlighting the darkness within. It is as if, in its terminal condition, the motel was declaring that in its twilight days it was still game to do what it always had, that is, providing hospitality to tired travelers.

In summers, up and down the Peninsula, motel populations swell with happy vacationers on their way east and south, "downee ocean" as the locals say. Cars are packed with bags and toys for the beach while kids ask, "Are we there yet?" or whine, "I have to go to the bathroom." They are all seeking the sun and fun of the Maryland and Delaware coastline. Folks come from Baltimore, Washington, D.C., Philadelphia, and other cities. For the last several years they will have passed an abandoned motel just north of Easton and never seen it, in the way a motorist's eyes hardly notice roadkill. After a while, long drives inure motorists to the passing landscape—except for the more garish sights, like the enormous road signs up and down the Eastern Shore that display advertisements for restaurants, motels, and casinos.

The small abandoned motel north of Easton had its day—not even its sign remained—and the only functional witness left to honor its contribution to the life of past summer migrations to the Peninsula were its doors. The doors still hung on their frames, able to open and close. A few locks worked so some doors could still provide one of a door's most important historic functions, that is, to safely secure its inhabitants for the night.

For many, the word *motel* doesn't imply class as, say, the word *hotel* or *inn* does. Time dulls the hard edges of what antiquity once offered to travelers. The "inn" of colonial times may have provided you a bed, but no shower. Forget running water. You'd get a chamber pot or use an outside privy, and probably share your bed with strangers who'd hadn't changed their clothes in weeks. Our modern motels, however marginal, have a leg up on any inn of old. Comfort and the basic amenities trump class for most modern travelers. Even B&B's that trade in "the good old days" have central heating, bathrooms, and showers and provide AC, television, and wi-fi.

Of all the doors at the old motel, it was the one at room number 9 that enchanted me most. I imagined that the face of that door was like the faces of wise old men or women, with time telling a story in every wrinkle. And indeed the door face was heavily wrinkled and rippled with weathered wood and peeling paint. I wondered, as I watched shadows play around the curled folds of paint, what those stories may have been that the door had overheard, tales told by people who had once come by to stop and to rest on their journey downee ocean.

There are old men and women in our world who are full of years and whom time and circumstance have made increasingly invisible. People hardly notice them anymore, like doors. But they've seen it all, and heard hundreds of stories. Old doors are a little like that: The hinges on which they move are worn, stiff and creak some, but what they have learned of others in their lifetime they treat with discretion. They never tell. It's a part of age's wisdom.

THE TERRAIN

Chester River

AROUND THE BEND

I find that the boundaries of the open Bay and its tributaries are easily blurred; they merge together in my mind like images in a dream. I think it's because the Chesapeake Bay consists of so many tributaries: nineteen large rivers and at least four hundred smaller streams. When on the water, it's often hard to tell which is which. If I tell you I was out the other day on the Chesapeake Bay, the chances are good I was sailing on one of its rivers.

Since childhood I've found rivers mysterious. My grandfather skippered one of the excursion boats of the old Hudson River Day Line from Manhattan, up the Hudson River to Bear Mountain. On several occasions I sailed on his boat, the *Dewitt Clinton*.

The turns the river made excited me. Seeing a bend ahead, I became expectant, wondering what I might see, my state of anticipation growing as we moved ahead. I recall the feeling and I think the feeling was akin to joy, the sense one has that something wonderful is soon about to happen and the waiting gets filled with promise, the way a child feels on Christmas Eve.

We attribute magical properties to rivers. The mystique arises partly from the peculiar way rivers meander; they twist and turn unpredictably, wandering this way and that, as if their course were set by divine imperative rather than directed by an engineer's design.

Rivers, like stories, don't proceed in a straight line from beginning to end; if they did, they'd be boring. Their twists and turns keep me curious.

Rivers develop exotic legends. The Rhine, for example, is seductive; there, the temptress Lorelei lived, and with her golden hair and bewitching voice wooed hapless sailors, sending them crashing to their death on the rocks. Some rivers, like the Ganges, the Amazon, and the Nile, were accorded divine status; they were worshiped as gods. Jesus was baptized in the Jordan where God spoke to him, assuring him that he was his "beloved son." And the Greeks believed that human souls, on their final journey from this life to the netherworld, arrived by first passing over the dark waters of the River Styx.

I've seen the rivers of the Chesapeake transform surrounding landscapes, as if their wandering undulations had the power to cast spells. I know that on any river, the familiar landlocked world can be experienced as a very different place. Huckleberry Finn thought so on his epic journey down the Mississippi with his friend, Jim, the runaway slave. They were about some serious business on that trip, seeking freedom, while making marvelous discoveries. Lying in his canoe one night on the river, Huck observes, "The sky looks ever so deep when you lay down on your back in the moonshine. I never knowed it before. And how far a body can hear on the water such nights." I know what he means.

Anchored north of Oxford on the Tred Avon River shortly after sunset, I watched as the evening sky turned slowly from blue to black. Shooting stars darted here and there, like fireflies. I could hear the steady chorus of tree frogs and a solitary dog barking far away somewhere beyond a cornfield. It was a soothing sound, unlike the abrasive yapping of frantic dogs. It was a kind of lazy "woof" that sleepy dogs raise for the sheer pleasure of making sound, for the same reasons I suspect birds sing. When you're on a river around the Bay, the night sky not only "looks ever so deep," but the longer one watches, the bigger and deeper it becomes.

Geologists refer to the Bay as a drowned river, but I think the Chesapeake Bay is very much alive: if water is the blood of the Bay, rivers are the arteries. Mole, the voluble little critter of Kenneth Graham's classic, *The Wind in the Willows*, knew that rivers were alive: He saw the river as a full-bodied animal on a romp. If I say a river is going around the bend, I don't think it's going mad: I know it has a surprise waiting for me up ahead.

The first trip my wife, Jo, and I made up the Chester River was on a clear windless day. We motored. It was during the week and boat traffic was light. Somewhere up beyond Comegys Bight, the river made a turn and suddenly a panorama of sunflowers covering one bank exploded before us. Their color was set against the dark green foliage that served as a frame for them, and the sheer number of flowers seemed beyond reckoning. They wagged their yellow heads, sassy-like, as we motored by. Looking at the panorama, it seemed as if the whole scene pulsed, vibrated, with the kind of physical energy one sees in the brushstrokes Impressionist painters make. Coming upon the flowers was totally unexpected. We've returned over the years to cruise the river and see the sunflowers, but there's nothing that quite equals the adventure of a first discovery, especially on a river.

There are as many surprises below a river's surface as there are above it. I've been up and down the Tred Avon River and into its gunkholes a hundred times over the years. And so, one afternoon when returning from the Western Shore and making my way up the Tred Avon, I hardly expected anything remarkable. Something broke the surface on our starboard bow, and again at our stern. I was alarmed; I had no idea what was happening. Then I could see them, dolphins, several leaping from the water alongside our boat; they were in high spirits. They liked our sailboat, *Periplus*, and followed her, gamboling alongside us all the way to the red marker near Oxford, where they disappeared below the surface as suddenly as they'd appeared. I didn't know that dolphins live in the Bay. I was told later that, when the small fish become less available in the southern part of the Bay, dolphins wander up the Bay and into the rivers looking for food. On a river, you just never know what's next.

"What a jolly life," said the irrepressible Mole when he learned that Rat had always lived by a river. He could well have been speaking of the James, Potomac, Chester, Tred Avon, Choptank, or Sassafras Rivers when Rat replied, "It's my world . . . and I don't want any other. What it hasn't got is not worth having, and what it doesn't know is not worth knowing. Lord! The times we've had together."

Sacred Space

GUNKHOLES AND
SACRED SPACES

There's a small gunkhole off the Chester River, Reed Creek. I discovered it twenty-five years ago, by accident, while sailing up the Chester River. Gunkholes are the tiny creeks, harbors, and anchorages that are found everywhere along the Chesapeake. It was late in the day. I was tired and I wanted to settle in for the night. Reed Creek was the closest gunkhole.

The entrance was small, unmarked, and barely discernible from the river, but finally I spotted it. The entrance was narrow and shallow, and my cutter drew four and a half feet. I bumped and scraped my way in, hoping not to go aground, as the tide was ebbing and if I grounded the boat I'd be stuck fast in the channel for the night. Brother Carrera was right up to a point about deep water ports in the Bay, but getting to the safety of one means negotiating the shallows.

I made it in and anchored. The creek's location, a solitary and lovely place, was without a house in sight, with only an old tractor sitting in the surrounding field. The field stretched out before me into distant stands of trees. Hay and corn filled the field. The shoreline around the creek was eroding.

The erosion was exquisite in its transformation. The gradual reshaping of the land by the tide's ebb and flood left tree roots exposed and sun-bleached. They were twisted in a myriad of spectacular shapes, like bonsai trees, while the shifting muddy contours of the shoreline created tiny cliff-like precipices, with small hollows underneath in which I saw creeping things—a frog, a turtle. A few large insects scaled the tiny heights, like cliff climbers. The stillness was palpable. The silence demanded your attention like a loud shout might in other circumstances—and even though wind blew and treetops bent and swayed, the water remained motionless as if exempt from natural law.

In the safety of the gunkhole's deep water, I felt as if I were in sacred space. Why should I feel this way? This was no church, shrine, sanctuary, or temple built for the divine to inhabit. It was a tiny slice of tidewater, not atypical of the many along the shores of the Bay. Perhaps it was the time of day, the way the landscape breathed with solitude. Or was it my own momentary disposition, as if there had been a divine confluence of events to create my fleeting sense of the holy as it lives in me and in the natural world of which I'm part? This is what epiphanies are made of: a divine confluence of time, tide, and events in which we find ourselves, like the crossing parallels and meridians that locate us in space as we continue on our journey through time.

That evening at anchor I thought of the extensive erosion taking place in the creek. The present face of the shoreline was disappearing. Short of erecting a stone breakwater, nothing but a dried-up river would keep the land from being inevitably drawn back into the creek.

Which claims primacy in the ecological maze we call nature? Was the land here first and therefore might legitimately claim primogeniture? Was the water here from the beginning and therefore entitled to enjoy first claim on what happens in the neighborhood and can dictate what stays and what goes? In the natural world it's never either/or, but both/ and. There are millions of trade-offs, symbioses, cooperative arrangements creating an evolving landscape that today is here and tomorrow is gone while being made new by forces of which I know only few. I wished the creek would stay just as I had first seen it that day. I wanted to hold the holy still, to control it. I wanted to seize the moment in time and freeze it there so I could return again and again to savor the moment. However, even my presence on that July day was effecting changes, the changes science tells us about; how both the beholder and that which is beheld, in their mutual act of discovery, change each other. We are all lovers in the natural world, changing each other as we meet. We rarely know just how we will be changed. We're not always gentle lovers. In the end, though, everything passes and is made new.

A breakwater might save the shoreline, hold it still, I thought. But it would make this beautifully sculptured shoreline into a bastion, like ramparts of a fort, creating a rigid and unnatural boundary as if the land and water were natural adversaries and had to be kept far from one another. The boundaries of our spirits ebb and flood all the time. The tide of affairs constantly shapes and forges them so they may keep conforming to the inexorability of change. Some call it evolution. I prefer the word *becoming*.

I had already been changed in the reciprocal way in which simply beholding and being beheld alters things. Best to let the creek work its own way and best for me to thank God that I was there at just the right time to see the creek in its fullness and to be able to tell the story of what I saw.

Blackwater Refuge

'TWIXT THE MARSH AND THE SKIES

Marshes smell. They're slimy, wet, dirty, and filled with all kinds of creepy crawlies. Marshes are the glory of the Chesapeake Bay.

I grew up around marshes. On Staten Island we sometimes called the marshes "swamps." There, the word *swamp* carried a pejorative meaning, a repository of decay and wastes, because the marshes of Fresh Kills on Staten Island hosted New York City's infamous garbage dump. Normally marshes smell ripe but, where I grew up, they had the additional pong of rotting urban effluence.

By popular convention, I'm supposed to hold mountains in lofty esteem. They're above it all, as if certain landscapes could be haughty and stick their noses up in the air. A mountain is the venerable icon expressing nobility, purity, grandeur, and the hallowed site of spiritual awakenings, a site where Moses spoke with God and where he received the Ten Commandments.

I typically view mountains at great distances, an experience different from being on top. Mountaintops are freezing cold, with wind blowing a gale and air thin on oxygen. Mountaintops are mostly inhospitable to human or animal life. Swamps and marshes, on the other hand, are welcoming. Marshes are fecund, serving as womb to all kinds of living things. Moses made it to the mountaintop, yes, but only because he'd had a good start from the marshes.

The normally melancholy Book of Job is full of surprises. One is how Job reveres the critters we're more cautious of: "If you want to know the ways of God, the creeping things of the earth will give you lessons, and the fish of the sea provide you with an explanation." Tidewater country is an excellent place to get some explanations for what God's about.

We depend on marshes. Their creepy inhabitants are significant contributors to our food chain and, for some like me, the marshes provide sustenance for my spiritual life. In my estimation, a marshy epiphany is equal to if not more inspiring than any mountaintop experience.

Our colonial forebears were wary of swamps. They believed swamps bred illness and hosted evil spirits. These spirits came at night in the marshes, appearing as spectral undulations that glowed in the dark and scared the locals witless. "Will-o-the wisps" we know now are methane released by the decomposing detritus fermenting in swamp beds. The will-o-the wisp is perhaps a symbolic reminder that our moments of mystery, however lofty we regard them, are rooted as much in the down and dirty of this world as they are in the ethereal realms of the otherworldly. It's all about body and soul.

Marshes are a macrocosm of our bodies. Mixed feelings about our bodies are common: We'd just as soon not know about the creeping and slithering microscopic organisms traveling throughout them. We find our fetid discharges embarrassing, and natural aromas like sweat and bad breath noxious. The hardened particles of mucus that inhabit our noses we try extricating, but only secretly, or while driving, where anonymity is more possible since to acknowledge the presence of the substance openly to others is socially offensive. The stuff lurking just under our skin causes many of us, when by some accident we are exposed directly to it, to faint dead away.

Historically, clerics have admonished spiritual seekers, for their soul's health, to maintain "pure thoughts." We are told that cleanliness is next to godliness, to eschew filthy lucre and to live "spotlessly."

We're created a little lower than the angels, according to the Bible. In our first primal state, however, we were just algae and slime, and one science writer suggests we consisted of what collects in the traps of sink drains, pond surfaces, and tidal marshes. As we developed lungs and began moving from mud pool to mud pool, we finally drew the breath of life directly from heaven itself. Nevertheless, we were stuck in the mud for a long time.

Marsh critters enjoy their bodies. They know how to play. They're physically affectionate. The male crab is amorous. While his mate sheds her old shell, he embraces her until the process is complete and her new shell hardens.

My yoga teacher told me that when we learn to love our bodies, all aspects of them, from the least honorable parts to the most revered, we're happier and kinder to others. I've noticed people who love their bodies also love to play. Their delight is infectious, like a dancer's. There's an exception. Watch people running, "working out." Runners can be seen regularly on our Shore's country roads. Working out is for health and not usually for fun, and seeing a runner's agonized expression tells the story. Working out is to achieve an end, an improved product, and a stronger body; it's work, though. Playing is something else and often accomplishes what fitness freaks seek. Nature does it by playing.

In *The Wind and the Willows*, Kenneth Grahame tells us about one of his itinerant characters, Mole. Mole's at the water's edge, watching the stream, this *"sleek, sinuous, full-bodied animal, chasing and chuckling, gripping things with a gurgle and leaving them with a laugh, to fling itself on fresh playmates that shook themselves free, and were caught and held again. All was a-shake and a-shiver—glints and gleams and sparkles, rustle and swirl, chatter and bubble. The mole was bewitched, entranced, fascinated."* Grahame's classic is a poem of the marsh and the water's edge, where inhabitants weave in and out of each other lives in playful symphonic romps, like spiritual fugues made manifest.

One day in the marshes, not far from my house, I watched as ducks cavorted, and on another day, as otters played. Animals and birds play well, and I've often seen them in the marshes frolicking to a fare-thee-well. Animals and birds enjoy their bodies. They have fun while getting plenty of exercise.

Over the years I've noticed one lone amphibious creature that swam, with just his head surfaced, from the far shore of my creek to the other side. His short trip was at the same time each day, his course clearly determined, the trip impelled by a necessity other than for pleasure. I called him "the commuter." I found his dutiful attention getting to work the exception here in the creek; most critters just liked to play.

I was about to make coffee one morning and looked out the window to the creek, expecting to see the commuter. Instead, five otters were swimming in front of the dock. They swam languidly and sensuously as the water on their fir glistened silver-like in the early morning light, as if each were coated with mercury. They crisscrossed each other's paths unhurriedly, like swimmers in a water ballet so well practiced that every move they made appeared liquid-smooth and effortless. Otter over otter they slid in slow motion, and then made their way in ever-greater circles, thoroughly delighting in each other's touch, as they nuzzled and cuddled each other in their sleepy passes. One by one they finally disappeared below the water, and then as suddenly as they appeared, one day they were gone and I never saw them again.

Marshes abound with all kinds of birds, enjoying the best of both possible worlds, the one above the surface and the one below.

> *"Behold,"* wrote the poet Sydney Lanier,
> *I will build me a nest on the greatness of God:*
> *I will fly in the greatness of God as the marsh hen flies*
> *In the freedom that fills the space*
> *'twixt the marsh and the skies.*

Ducks love marshes; some species around the Chesapeake Bay are equally at home underwater, on land, at the surface, or airborne. "Divers" seem to have more fun than the "dabblers." "Dabblers" are the ducks that stay on the surface. They don't dive underwater. Of all the divers, I love best watching the mergansers and the buffleheads. The mergansers' crowns look like the heads of adolescent boys whose hair won't stay combed down. They shag straight out from the back of the heads unruly and wet. There were six of these mergansers in the marsh the other day paddling along like a Lilliputian armada. I think they were flirting. The males stretched their necks high, rocking backwards, and while not ascending to flight, flapped their wings furiously, slapping the water and sounding like drum rolls in slow motion. In unison they'd dart to the right and left, turn around, come directly at each other on a collision course, then veer to the side just shy of impact. The females watched their suitors' antics with eagerness, egging them on with responsive, reactive motions, like small spasms. Then some, as if weary of the game, dove under the water.

Next they all developed a diving frenzy. First they'd strut, patter about on the surface, feint to one side then another, and then dive. This dive wasn't jerky, like jack-knifing from a springboard; it was more like a roll, a fluid-like somersault, as dolphins do, smooth as satin. Two or three of the ducks would disappear below the surface of the water. Mergansers will usually surface nearby. As they each dove I'd play a game; I'd bet myself I could predict exactly where they would surface. Not once did I ever guess correctly. I figured they were just teasing me. And, as if there were more joy inside them than their tiny bodies were able to contain, the ducks reverenced their Creator in as stunning a rite as any celebrated in the most glorious liturgies of the world; they dove, strutted, stretched, fussed, and flapped, dipped, then finally rose again, ascending and flying away until they were lost to sight somewhere "twixt the marsh and the sky."

Nettles

GOING WITH THE FLOW

Nettles—also known as "jellyfish" here—get a bad rap. Spineless, they say, nothing but drifters, and so transparent you can see right through them. They foul water intakes on motorboats. They sting. Kids call nettles icky. Don't be fooled. Nettles are not without resolve, nor do they want for purpose. For all their transparency they remain profoundly mysterious, and despite their gelatinous consistency and prickly stringers they're as hardy as cockroaches and as stunning as flowers. Nettles have been here almost as long as there has been life. There's a lesson here somewhere.

I anchored one morning on the Tred Avon River on a hot August day. On the ebb tide, large nettles were gliding ghostlike past my boat. They go with the flow.

The morning clouds reflected on the water's surface. The nettles hovered just below the surface. They slid lithely along in the murky water, undulating slightly, their stringers trailing along looking like the tails of comets at twilight. They were a sight to see, a look at a prehistoric creature relatively unchanged by time, roughly 650 million years.

I like to think that nettles survive because they have made peace with the world without demanding that it be other than it is. There's something to be said in living life below the surface while knowing how to go with the flow.

In the middle of the nineteenth century, scientists became intrigued with the abyss, as the depths of the ocean were then called. They searched ocean floors with long cables and drew from the darkness all kinds of exotic creatures. A prevailing theory held that the soft gelatinous slime covering the ocean floor was the stuff from which all life proceeded. Woolly mammoths, as well as roses and parakeets, could be traced back to the primal ooze that covered the earth's seabeds. A theory some entertained was that many of the life forms that couldn't accommodate to surface life eventually found their way to the bottom of the ocean. Having made adaptations, they were believed transformed and living on in the lightless depths. Plumbing the abyss might not only teach us where we came from, but where we'll wind up.

I used to think heaven was the place where answers to life's imponderable questions were to be found, questions like Why am I here? Where will I finally go? I was here, I thought, and God was up above. Any answers I'd receive would be directed from up there.

I have always had a peculiar attitude in prayer; instead of closing my eyes and bowing my head, as preachers invite us to do, I prefer looking skyward with my eyes wide open; I don't want to miss a thing. That underwater, below the surface, there might be as many opportunities for spiritual awakening as there were up in the sky had never occurred to me—except once. In church, I first heard the tale of Jonah and his three-day sojourn in the abyss. It didn't change him much—he still had something of an attitude—but he took stock and changed some. In my own search for meaning, the thought of what goes on below the surface as another locus of revelation widened my horizons: My spirit might be fed with what's below the surface as well what's way out there.

Most nettles go with the flow, but we, a terminally restless breed, don't. We flit from one thing to another, one idea to the next, seeking satisfaction by staying in motion, but the satisfaction eludes us each time.

For me, the restlessness is like hunger, the kind that nothing I can imagine will satisfy. I look up to the clouds, or at what's below me, like a flower maybe, or a turtle. From the corner of my eye, a small part of our creation arrests my attention as it did on the morning I watched nettles go with the flow in an ebbing tide. Suddenly the restlessness stops and my spirit is sated, at least for while.

Food for the spirit like that isn't gathered. It's delivered right to my door wherever I might be. Best just to wait, stay alert—and eventually it finds me. It's really a matter of becoming aware of what's right under my nose, the way manna once appeared seemingly out of nowhere to a hungry people lost in a desert. It was the last thing they expected to see in such a place.

There are, I noticed, restless nettles. For these few, going with the flow is difficult. These are nettles with itchy protoplasm, so to speak. I saw one that morning in the Tred Avon River drifting past my sailboat.

He was a particularly large and meaty nettle, and beat the crown of his bell repeatedly against the surface of the water. He seemed uncharacteristically fidgety. Remaining obstinately vertical, propelling himself upward from below again and again, his bell broke the surface of the water only slightly, leaving a transient ripple. As he began to sink below, with the same steady undulations as his cousins were performing to move horizontally and with the flow, he'd attempt the same gyrations, but striving for a vertical ascent; I think he was reaching for the sky. Even with high hopes he could only do so much and was able to break the surface ever so little. It must have been maddening for him, as though he were trying to break through a transparent ceiling that constrained his life, the way I've heard women speak of the restraint the culture often places on their aspirations. He was trying for a peek at a world beyond him, for a glimpse of the universe of which he was a part, but could not participate because of constraints.

What drives such determination? That same restlessness that from the beginning of the human race has driven us: It's the same restlessness that makes some of us long to reach the stars, to explore the abyss, and to break the glass ceiling. We want to know where we came from, where we will go, accomplish and to see the face of God. For a short time that morning on the Tred Avon River, both above and below, it was enough for me that day just going with the flow.

Oyster

OSTREIDA AND HOMO SAPIENS

Once, during an exceptionally low tide, I walked out on my dock. In every direction, I saw oyster shells. The Chesapeake Bay abounds in oysters, even today despite the environmental assaults they've endured. I stood there for a moment and wondered how the species survived as long as it has, perhaps as long as 520 million years, well before we arrived. No matter where in the world they're found, oysters belong to one family. Families that stick together survive longer than ones that don't.

By the values I normally hold for the life worth living, I must say that oysters would seem poor candidates for survival. They have no get-up-and-go. They're hard-edged, and should you get too close and pry, they clam up. They lie around, stuck in the mud, and drink all the time. They possesses an extraordinarily eclectic sexuality: One day a boy decides to be a girl, and the next day prefers being a boy again and both sexes have the wherewithal to switch sides. God imparted eccentricities in abundance to the oyster, and not the social graces, industry, beauty, and sexual propriety I associate with being just folks.

Still, oysters play a part in the divine scheme of things in the same way some acquaintances I've known who give little thought to cleanliness, are uncommunicative, hard-edged, heavy drinkers, and even sexually capricious. Either way, like oysters, we all belong to one family and everyone serves a function in the larger scheme of things. My entrenched attitudes of entitlement and exclusivity tend to obscure the reality of my interdependence with all beings.

Until the beds were closed in 1927 because of pollution, my ancestors were active for at least four generations in New York Harbor's lucrative oyster trade. My father was tight-lipped on this matter for unknown reasons and never mentioned it. I found out about it by accident, on one of my boyhood visits to my grandmother's house. She told me after I'd asked her about the starfish that sat next to an oyster shell on an end table.

I thought the starfish was more exotic, but as she explained the adversarial relationship between starfish and oysters—they kill oysters by drilling holes in their shells—I learned about the rise and fall of the oyster business that belonged to my great-grandfather John I. Merrill and his father before him. They ran an oyster and fish market on Fulton Street in New York City.

Oysters never appeared at our table when I was growing up. In 1965, as a young man, I was in New Orleans and I ordered oysters Rockefeller, my first oysters. I loved them. Not until 1974 in Maryland did I eat my first raw oyster from the Bay.

Oysters Rockefeller disguise an oyster's native character some, concealing the gnarled and pitted shell in rock salt while cloaking its gelatinous essence with spinach, onion, spice parisienne, and absinthe. The fixings made eating oysters Rockefeller easy. Presentation helps a lot. Eating raw oysters, however, was more challenging; there is only the oyster, no frills, man to mollusk. But once I ate what looked like such forbidden fruit, I was hooked and now I love oysters raw, fried, or baked. I also think oysters are beautiful and their peculiar habits and physiognomy make a prophetic statement.

The shell of the raw oyster is as mysterious as the food and liquor it contains. After I ate my first raw oyster, I held the shell up to the light, turning it this way and that, the way I do entertaining a new thought.

The shell looked primal, as ageless as the sea, alluring like a jewel. It was grey and felt stippled and rough to the touch like Braille. A few tiny barnacles had made their home on the shell along with a couple of sea worms. This oyster's home had provided hospitality to neighbors in the mixed neighborhood in which it once lived. I could see that the oyster's striated armor had been meticulously formed, layer upon layer, laid up like ceramic tiles on a roof. Although the shell's exterior was gnarled and beaten, the inside was decidedly uptown. The oyster's living space revealed a miniature palace, a salon fully glazed and satin smooth. The pearl-like patina of its walls was accented with occasional splashes of blue. The interior formed a seamless sanctuary where the oyster could rest safely ensconced as cozily as though it were royalty reclining between pillows of silk. The oyster is as remarkable a creature as we are. There's one difference; oysters are not predatory.

"All true oysters, regardless of where they are found, belong to the family Ostreida," writes Mark Kurlansky in his book, *The Big Oyster: History on the Half Shell*. The outward appearances of human beings, like oysters, vary considerably, but they are nonetheless members of one family. Sadly, unlike oysters, we frequently fight each other and can't seem to stick together like families should.

Sculpture

OWLS AND OSPREYS

Every year in Easton, here on the Easton Shore, we celebrate the Waterfowl Festival. It's a gala three-day affair, held in the fall to coincide with the annual migrations of geese. Local and national artists exhibit their work, hunting skills and dog retriever demonstrations are held. There's a goose-calling competition, decoy carving, and conservation exhibits. Local foods such as oysters and crabs are on offer. My church sponsors a food booth: I volunteer to help sell oysters at our booth because the local shucker, an African American waterman, can shuck ten oysters to my one. He gives me as many as I want to eat.

A few years ago, at the Waterfowl Festival I saw an exhibit that featured three owls that had been sculpted from metal. I found them striking because the negative spaces, as well as the metal fabrications, formed their image. The visual impact was stronger for the presence of the empty space.

"For it is only framed in space that beauty blooms. Only in space are events and objects and people unique and significant—and therefore beautiful," writes Anne Morrow Lindbergh in her classic, *Gifts from the Sea.*

Managing space creatively is the nature of art, and a survival skill, too. Empty space is slowly ebbing away through human migrations and by economic development.

Recently, at night I've begun hearing the squawks of a screech owl around Broad Creek. It's a disagreeable sound, petulant, whiney, not like the great horned owl that once lived in the woods surrounding our house. His mellifluous "who hoo" filled the night air with a melancholy, haunting echo, the way the sounds of a cello fill a concert hall. I miss him.

One morning I noticed an osprey swooping down on a section of woods by the creek. He persisted. I went for a closer look. Sure enough, the screech owl was sitting in a tree, too close to the osprey's nest. The osprey was telling the owl to buzz off.

Why had I never heard a screech owl when the great horned owl lived nearby? A naturalist told me that screech owls keep away from great horned owls because they'll attack them. For unknown reasons the great horned owls left the neighborhood, thereby making space for screech owls.

For years I'd see quail in our yard. Then the house next door was sold. New owners cleared the lot of underbrush and manicured their lawn meticulously like golf greens. The quail, their home destroyed, disappeared.

Accommodating one another in limited space is as daunting for humans as it is for quail, owls, and ospreys. The immigration debate reveals the issue as does a conversation about racial equity. There is an irony in the conversation. From the beginning, America was built by émigrés, including slaves. No one except Native Americans can claim to be an American whose ancestors had not come from elsewhere. They are the ones whom the newly arrived émigrés quickly routed, just as my neighbor had the routed the quail, or the osprey the screech owl.

The Eastern Shore's Hispanic population is growing rapidly. I've often wondered what must it be like to leave the familiar space of your own land for economic survival and come to the Delmarva, where you don't speak the language, know the local mores or even the regional food. It must be a lonely and a difficult task, finding safe space where one can feel at home. One of the greatest challenges facing human survival is our capacity to mutually regulate our differences and to find space for one another. It's particularly challenging in Maryland today; although a small state, it is one of the more populous in America.

Economic success has been the icon of the American myth. Lionizing success, however, obscures the spiritual underpinning of the American dream, symbolized by the Statue of Liberty. It's a symbol of hospitality, welcoming the stranger and offering refuge and space. Hospitality, perhaps the oldest social and religious convention, is still observed, but, interestingly, we see it exercised more among the poor of the Third World than the affluent of the West.

Birds can't think beyond survival. We can. An old saying invites us to "Welcome the stranger for you may be entertaining angels unawares." It's worth doing; you never know who'll show up.

Leaf

RAIN WHISPERS

Trappist Monk Thomas Merton once wrote: "Nobody started it, nobody is going to stop it. It will talk as long as it wants, this rain. As long as it talks, I am going to listen." Listen to rain? April, on the Eastern Shore, is a good time to keep your ear to the ground, to hear not only the rain speak, but the earth, too.

It's a curious thought about water, but one possible reading of the Book of Genesis suggests that water existed even before God created light. The reading: "A wind from God swept over the face of the waters," assumes water is already here before the command "Let there be Light" was issued. Science and religion usually agree that creation began with light. We can't live without the earth, water, or light and since we've now got all of them here on the Shore, however it came down, it's worked out well.

It rained hard one April some years ago and I was put out about it. Outside chores needed doing and rain was preventing me. I feel out of control when anything interferes with my plans.

I began to notice how, when the rain fell, it fell with a sound like a whisper or a soft wind. In the afternoon, the rain stopped for a while and I went outside to walk around. The trees and shrubs were dripping. The front yard was soaked. The ground made a strange bubbly sound, like seltzer water being freshly poured into a glass. The voice sparkled. I thought it was the voice of the earth.

Was this a conversation with earth initiated by the clouds miles above? I know the earth and the clouds, the raindrops and the soil, and I—we're all of a piece—are neighbors in this cosmic community. Had I overheard my neighbors speaking with each other, one in a whisper, and the other with a bubbly and vivacious voice? I didn't understand a word being said. I was getting the message, though. They knew each other well. They enjoyed some kind of intimate relationship.

The rain resumed, continuing steadily, whispering softly. It stopped intermittently and I'd go out into the yard to listen for the sparkling sound of the earth. I'd incline my head, like a robin. I listened as the earth spoke.

I was familiar with the soft sounds of falling rain, but never had I heard earth speak.

Hushed voices always grab my attention more than the loud shouts. I can't resist trying to hear conversations in a crowd carried on in whispers. It's particularly inviting since the exchange seems so exclusive, intimate, and secretive. I strain to listen to the gossip. I don't want to be left out.

The rain had curtailed the normal busyness of my frantic life and slowed me down sufficiently to begin to listen for rain whispers and the earth's effervescent reply. I held my breath. I didn't want to miss a word, nor a single note. In one sense I had entered another world, although it was the same one I've lived in all my life. More to the point, I listened to my world in ways I had not before. Rain forced me to stop, cancelling plans for the day, but, rather than confining me as I'd first feared, rain freed me up to be with my world in a new way.

A cold front came through. Soon the hushed world shook with roars of thunder and streaks of lightning as the rain made its exit from the stage in a blaze of glory. After the rain my world smelled clean and sweet for a while, like a baby fresh from a bath.

The sun came out. It felt warm on my face. Humidity returned and I could smell vegetation—as I often can on the Delmarva after storms. I always imagined that it happened that way in the Garden of Eden after a rain. There, rivers and lush foliage were once reported to have been abundant everywhere.

CRITTERS

Birds on a Wire

FOR THE BIRDS

Driving to Salisbury on Rt. 50, I noticed birds perched on top of the wires between utility poles, hunkered down like sports fans at a stadium. Why there, instead of in trees or shrubs where birds normally gather?

They like the high ground, I first thought. It offers them better views of us doing what we humans do most of the time: driving our cars back and forth. They're watching us, like birders watch birds. I notice that birds remain out in the open as if they had no secrets to keep or malicious intents. Birders, on the other hand, hide in the brush, peeking out, furtively, like burglars or cats.

The birds looked tense, beaks high and tails straight as ramrods. A few were interested more in romance than in watching cars, like singles who join bird watchers, not for observing birds but to find a significant other. I say that because here and there along the wires, I'd see just two birds snuggled together, beak to cheek, totally enthralled with each other.

Birds can't really be people watchers, though, as car drivers would be invisible to the birds and Rt. 50 has few if any pedestrians. They must be watching the cars. If I were close enough to the birds and could translate, might I hear something like "There goes a tail-gater," or "See that one over there? It's an Edsel! I thought they were extinct." But why would cars interest birds at all?

Birds have been here over 150 million years, while we've been here only a million and a half. Cars and interstates are new arrivals. Birds may once have been curious about us and about our cars, but the novelty has surely worn off by now. I'll bet the birds are anxious about the sheer numbers of cars we drive. We're poisoning their neighborhood. We are poisoning our neighborhood.

In the fall, blackbirds invade the Eastern Shore in mind-boggling numbers. They swarm like bees, darkening the horizon like storm clouds in undulating columns that rotate like tornadoes. The blackbirds land in trees around my house and chatter incessantly. The noise is deafening. I whack a cast iron skillet with a spoon; the noise sends them screaming off. Their sheer numbers, their chatter, and the indiscriminate dumping of their waste I find intolerable.

Maybe birds are similarly disturbed by what we do: millions of cars and trucks invading their space, and the relentless noise and toxic emissions they generate. Birds must feel as I did when the blackbirds appeared overhead. I could drive them away by making noise. The birds, however, are helpless against the onslaught of cars. They can't do a thing.

They watch helplessly as cars and trucks pass by under them in overwhelming legions, intruding on the tranquility of their countryside and filling their beaks and our skin-thin atmosphere with carbon monoxide. Cars may have once intrigued birds, but no more. Now they're scared.

I saw no birds on my drive last week. It bothered me. Had they abandoned their protest against our environmental abuses? I hope not. Who'd be left to remind us that the way we're managing our air quality is for the birds?

Indecision

GOOSE TALES

Geese, like many boaters and tourists who show up on the Shore, are seasonal visitors. They stay for a while and then leave. Like me, most retirees stay . . . as long as they can.

Whether arriving, taking off, or just floating around, geese make an extraordinary ruckus. One night in the fall some years ago, while we anchored on the Wye River near Shaw Bay, a huge colony of geese settled in the water near us. I was unable to hear what my wife was saying across the cockpit for the din that the geese were making. Geese generate thunderous volume because they all talk at once the way anxious people do. Why so much to say? I have no idea, unless, perhaps, as frequent fliers, they're relieved to have arrived safely and enjoy telling each other stories of where they've been, the ups and downs of their flight south, and who they'd bumped into along the way. I heard a lot of stories that night; I couldn't sleep a wink.

Once, in late spring, I woke in the middle of the night to the honking of a solitary goose. I'm used to the sounds that gaggles of geese make. It's odd hearing only one goose. I felt melancholy listening. I couldn't get back to sleep, but not because of the noise—the honking wasn't intrusive—but for the suggestion of what this plaintive voice might portend.

In spring I'm expecting nature's new arrivals, but not geese. They're gone by spring. This goose must have been around the Bay since the fall, anyway. I doubt it was a recent arrival. To hear the honking of only one goose when I know that he or she, only a month ago, was surrounded by the convivial chatter of friends and relatives, inclines me to think the worst: perhaps its spouse died or for health reasons the goose wasn't up to making the long trip north. For this goose, spring was not a beginning, but an end.

There are gains and losses in the seasons of life. I think of the retirees who come to the Shore to live out their days in the gentle ambience of tidewater country. In my community most of the people are of riper years, most over fifty-five. The days of contentment endure for a while, but then there's the inevitable illness and death. One of the couple remains to live out the dream they both once shared.

Not far from my home just off the Bozman-Neavitt Road, a couple I knew once named their home "Final Decision." The name was inscribed on a plaque attached to a covered well housing that stood by the road. The home is still there, the well housing too, but the name has disappeared.

"Final Decision" was a word play on the husband's profession—he had been a judge—and implied that this was the last move the couple planned to make. In short, like many here, they came to live out their lives on the Shore. The husband died and the wife stayed on in the house. After some years she became disabled with age and her family saw the necessity of moving her to a facility providing regular care. After she left, the sign began losing letters, falling off one by one, until, when I last saw the sign, the remaining letters read like the word *indecision*. The life decisions we make are rarely final; they're tentative. The final decision is made elsewhere.

I considered another possible scenario to account for the solitary bird's presence. Indeed, like Henry David Thoreau, the goose's election of solitude may have been a statement. He'd had it with the noise, the crowded skies, congestion on the creeks, geese everywhere flapping and fussing, and hours in the air. The goose found his own Walden Pond, on the creek in front of my house.

The world presents trade-offs to man and goose alike. It's comforting to know that someone's nearby. It's also important to have time and space to be still and alone. To be assured of the comforts and safety that companionship and society provide, most species congregate together in one way or another. For our part, we build and inhabit homes around the tranquil coves we love, sail the open waters that beckon us, and drop our hooks in the silent creeks and rivers that promise us a night's safe anchorage. But we also insist upon having conveniences nearby like shopping malls with big boxes. We profane the very pristine nest we sought for refuge, the place where we found gentle space, where we could engage in the discernment that solitude brings, and where that soft, downy texture of stillness can be heard, the stillness that cradles the soul like soft pillows sooth sleepy heads.

After a month or so I never saw the goose again. Who knows where he'd gone? But I like to think that he went on searching for that perfect time that includes discovering the uncommon place for which many of us longed and which we found for a while on the Shore.

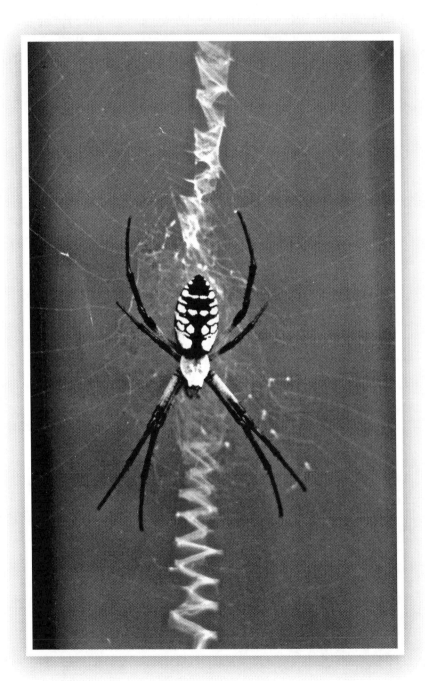

Spider

WWW. WEBS

The Eastern Shore is home to thousands of insects. Some are lovely, like the monarch butterfly. Lots are pesky, like the mosquito, and a few, like the deer tick, can be dangerous. Others, however, are simply stunning like the large garden spiders, one of which lives just outside my kitchen door.

Variously named, these spiders are also called writer spiders. They inscribe on their webs a unique signature that looks like seam stitching. I see her now all the time as I come and go. Her size—almost an inch long, and a good two inches with legs extended—along with her stunning yellow and black colors, immediately draws my eye. The spider is always located at her web's center, stone still with her head down. This writer spider has been there for three weeks at least, and with a few modifications she's made in her web from time to time, it looks as if she plans being there in the same way for the duration. The writer spider is remarkably patient. She spends her life weaving and waiting.

To make a web requires ingenuity and high-tech savvy, but especially patience; her task is fraught with hazards. Webs are almost invisible, and people walk into them all the time. I have twice, accidentally. Wind may rend the webs apart, as do heavy rains, and sometimes the connections are so fragile that they break on their own.

Birds can also do in the webs. In short, food shopping for spiders is an uncertain task that requires hours of waiting and frequent disappointments. If nothing else, spiders hang in there.

The sheer marvel of these webs made me curious about spiders and for more information one day I went online, namely, to www. webs.org, .net, and then. com. The first sites I hit made no reference to spiders. It surprised me. Spiders have been creating websites long before we ever arrived on the planet or had an alphabet. They've been at it for about three hundred and ninety-five million years. We've been engaged in the practice of using webs seriously since about 1993 and I began learning the computer and browsing the web only a few years ago. For prehistoric Arachnids and the postmodern Homo sapiens, the web is a way of life.

For spiders, the web puts food on the table. For man the Web serves a related function-selling products—but also sharing information with others. Unlike spiders, we're definitely more social animals and so we design personal websites. They tend to be exhibitionistic and have a more narcissistic quality to them, but they also share information.

Both writers and spiders create webs by various kinds of spin and can at times weave tenuous connections. Sometimes our webs net little by way of substance. The connections in the spider's case consist of gossamer threads of silk, which the spider produces in her glands—creating one strand by merging many, like laid-up line, and then weaves them into an intricate pattern. Unlike our webs, all of theirs are designed for one purpose—to eat. How a spider gets her web up and running, however, is extraordinary.

Many years ago, in Royal Oak, a village here on the Eastern Shore, I sat on a dock watching a sunset. Because it was protected from the wind by a thick stand of trees, the water lay still and tranquil. I saw that a spider had managed to string a single thread from one piling to another and from there construct a web. The pilings were at least ten feet apart. The strand was imperceptible—I would never have seen it—except it was laden with beads of evening moisture, which caught the sun's late light. The lone strand looked like a garland of tiny diamond chips—"of the first water" as jewelers might say—strung together by an invisible thread. For years I kept wondering how she could have spanned the pilings to make the web. But that was before I learned to browse the Web.

After seeing the writer spider, I went online to learn what spiders like this were about, and sure enough, there it was: Spiders let out an initial strand to connect two locations. The strand is secured at one site while the other end is let to ride free in the breeze. An adhesive substance at that end sticks to whatever it first touches. Surfing webs for my spider cousin and for me as a writer is similar: It begins with being at loose ends and making an excursion into space in an attempt to tie something down.

The writer spider, at least the one I saw, stays on its web 24/7. It's tedious just hanging out there, waiting. Not everything she gets is welcomed, either, like leaf fragments, scraps of paper, splinters of plastic, dust, and inedible bugs. Just having a web out there attracts junk.

She has her problems with spam, but nothing like ours. When I get on the Web in the morning, my e-mail contains at least five to ten offers from solicitors from the United Kingdom or Africa. Some address me affectionately as "Beloved" or "Dearest," apologize for their unsolicited communication, wish me good health, and say they have been waiting to issue me a million pounds from an unclaimed bank account in Nigeria and have been instructed to distribute the contents to me. Why me? I have no clue. A sweet-talking lawyer is one thing, but one who calls you "Dearest" and says he has a million pounds to give you is quite another. Suspicion is warranted. The garden spider may have a leg up on us here. She doesn't run scams (well, maybe a couple).

Among the theories offered for the peculiar zigzag stitching writer spiders weave, one is that it acts as a kind of protective shield, a firewall of sorts. The theory goes that it may trick predators by confusing them, while inviting more promising prospects for dinner like moths and wasps. That the garden spider always keeps a head down may also suggest that this attitude works better than ours, where folk wisdom advises us that we keep a heads-up for avoiding unwelcome surprises or to get things done properly. Sadly, we cannot know the minds of arachnids. Their experience might prove invaluable in minimizing intrusions and improving efficiency, especially for writers. Spiders know: They've been successfully getting the bugs out of their own work for eons. We depend on editors. A part of me identifies with the writer spider. While trying to create essays, I spend a lot of time rooted in the same spot, head down, waiting for something to come to me while frequently winding up writing stuff that is inscrutable. Another problem is that I am not a computer natural and I have little confidence when on the Web. When a "fatal error" warning causes me self doubt, my first response is to hang it up.

Spiders still weave webs as they have for millennia. Arachnids are sending us a clear message. The lesson here is patience. When people mess up a spider's web or when the wind or the rain destroys her hard-earned creation, she shows no rancor. She's not retributive, nor does she become despondent. A writer spider doesn't hang it up, regale the universe, or develop an entitled attitude because of the reversals she suffers. She simply begins again.

She has learned that if she maintains her connections and waits patiently, in time what she needs most will find her. It works that way for writers, too.

St. Francis

THE EARTH SHALL TEACH THEE

I read once how in 1743 Henry McAllister, a resident of the town of Oxford, complained that his neighborhood was "swarming with bugs, Musketoes, worms of every sort both land and water, Spiders, Snakes, Hornets, Wasps, Sea Nettles, Ticks, Gnats . . . irregularities in abundance." He was not, as the saying goes, a happy camper.

I deal regularly with all kinds weather, insects, and other wildlife. It goes with the territory. However, with modern amenities, like screens, chemical resources such as insecticides, and caulking for cracks and holes in walls and basements, I enjoy greater control over intrusive pests than Mr. McAllister did. Today, like lawyers, exterminators are as close as my phone so I can be particular about the bugs I tolerate.

A passage in the Book of Job reads: "Speak to the earth and it will teach thee." Its lessons are easier to accept for people like me who are less vulnerable to the great outdoors. I also enjoy the benefits of leisure, a luxury that many earlier residents didn't have as they were scrambling for survival. I can reflect on the wonders of ecology with some impunity. On a hot afternoon recently, my wife, Jo, and I sat on the patio. We watched ants.

There were large ants and tiny ants. The tiny ones walked mostly in single file, like soldiers on parade. The big ones, however, darted back and forth, bumping into one another, as if frantically looking for something they'd lost and had only seconds to find it. Some ants seemed to be casting unusually large shadows. Looking closely I could see that those ants were each carrying another ant. It did not seem like predatory behavior, nor amorous, for that matter, but they were about some business that I didn't understand. The ants continued going in circles while they toted their burden. Eventually the toting ants went beyond the perimeter of the patio. I never saw what became of them.

Before the last toting ant walked away, I gently flicked one with my finger. I wanted to see what would happen. He dropped the ant he was carrying. Both ants seemed disoriented and started running in circles, but neither located the other. They bumped into other ants, checking them out the way dogs sniff out new acquaintances. When they realized it wasn't the ant they were looking for, they quickly resumed their search. I never saw the separated ants reunited again, but Jo reported seeing a pair find each other. Of course they had a plan, as nature would have it, but I had no idea what it was. For them, getting on one another's backs was apparently acceptable behavior. Getting off someone's back was not.

Physician, essayist, and biologist Lewis Thomas discusses how termite and ant behaviors differ. In community, termites live happy and productive lives. They drink little water (better for them) and watch their weight. While they're never preoccupied with sex, they love touching each other constantly, reaching out regularly with their antennae to affectionately nudge family and friends. Some, however, pair off and spurn the community to go it alone. They immediately stop touching each other. Curiously, they become keenly interested in sex, but it does nothing to enhance their relationship. In fact, they're so contentious that if another termite tries to get close to them, they'll bite its head off. Compulsive drinking (water) develops and they gain weight. This is different behavior from that of ants that never consider life outside the community.

Ants, Thomas tells us, like human beings, are social creatures. Ants together erect bridges with scientific precision, burrow tunnels deep underground, build houses from sand or mud, and cordon off rooms. They communicate with each other although their numbers may reach millions in any given colony. Ants swim and climb and a few even fly. Ants forage efficiently for food (like your sugar bowl), feed one another, raise huge families, and have a hierarchy that keeps order and discipline but allows each member to exercise his or her particular gifts. Ants know north from south, can follow the sun, will raise armies, fight wars, but also make peace. They will always remain connected to the earth even while checking out some child's abandoned half-eaten candy bar left in a room on the second floor of your house. They won't stay, but go back home after eating and taking a few morsels along for the road.

In short, ants make it big-time in this world not because each one strives to outdo the other, or one group of the colony insists its way is the only way, but because they stay connected to the earth of their origins and perhaps most significantly remain in constant communication.

Ants have learned the art of community, cooperation, and the humility that comes from remembering where you come from and not trying to be a celebrity. I wonder if their remarkable solidarity and industry and their success as a species in overcoming horrendous obstacles may have something to do with the fact—and I have no way of proving this—that it is a female that runs the show.

Remembering who you are, where your roots are, stabilize us in tackling daily life. Keeping our feet squarely on the ground provides us stability and a sense of connection. Keeping our feet on the ground may, in the long haul, be worth our lives if we are anything like ants. We are as communal a set of earth's critters as God ever made.

Thomas notes how two million army ants from Central America had once been transported to America and exhibited as an art form in a New York City gallery. Encased in a large plastic exhibit space, the ants were provided food, dirt, and water. They were well above ground in an upper floor, completely separated from the natural earth; the building with its concrete and steel foundations was at least twice removed from the ground.

In a short time the ants became sluggish and died, all two million of them, and were unceremoniously carted away to a dump. Their deaths remained a mystery and Thomas wonders whether toxins in the plastic display case may have done them in. I wonder, however, if the ants, which live intimately with the earth, really can't live apart from where they come from.

Perhaps the influx of people to the Shore wishing to live closer to the earth are hoping to bring new energy and meaning to their lives by returning to their roots, the plain earth, of which the Shore still has a good bit—although it's slowly disappearing from under our feet in the grand development schemes of the postmodern era.

Here and there I've noticed arrivals to the Shore who seem more like termites than ants; they construct large dwellings but live solitary lives and have no interest in the larger community. The closed gates and "No Trespassing" or "Private Property" signs may be indications of a different, less communal species showing up, digging in and wishing to be left alone.

Hour Glass

TIME FLIES

A plague of flies visited the Eastern Shore last fall. Judging from their shape and size, I assumed they were some species of horse fly. I have never seen so many.

I first noticed them in August. The flies measured about three quarters of an inch to an inch, gray in color with big heads and enormous compound eyes. They darted at breakneck speeds, like barn swallows. The flies exhibited unnatural behavior. They chased cars.

I came down the driveway one day. A squadron of the flies circled my car like buzzards over a carcass, not with the soaring grace of hawks, but with the speed and determination of hornets. Some struck the windshield with such force that they ricocheted off the glass like pebbles tossed up by passing cars. Bloodied but not bowed, the same flies quickly returned, coming at my windshield repeatedly, like fighter planes engaged in dogfights. Others careened downward, smacking onto the hood from sorties originating from high above. A few flies followed alongside the car as though escorting me, an oddly solicitous gesture from bugs hardly known for their hospitality.

I parked and got out of my car. A couple of flies buzzed me for a few seconds. None bit me. Soon they flew off. I realized that they thought my car was hot, not me. For these insects, the sport was in the chase.

Friends tell me that attributing to animals, birds, and insects human inclinations is unscientific, even childish. Nevertheless, I'm addicted to humanizing nature. Anthropomorphism unleashes my imagination and my mind takes off on hopelessly wild excursions. These strange flies seized my fancy. What did their behavior mean?

It was not as if I were driving a sexy muscle car or a pricey Jaguar. In fact the car I drive—my children tease me about it, calling it Dad's "old lady car"—is a Buick LaSabre and almost nine years old. Why exactly were the flies curious about my Buick? It may have been because, like me, the car was old, but still running.

Flies have a short life span. They're anxious as most of us are about longevity; looking, as I often have, for secrets of a longer life. Most flies live a month, some less. In this brief span they mate, raise families, forage for food, pester people and animals, and then die. This is a hard life. Squandering it chasing cars seems foolish.

This was not my first experience with the curious habits of flies. In my kitchen every August, one or two fruit flies will appear, usually on a banana peel. They have remarkably varied tastes. By mid-September the fruit flies are feeding everywhere. I'll find some in the shower on a bar of soap, others clinging to bath towels, still others buzzing old tuna fish cans, and, for an elite few, when late in the day my wife and I enjoy a drink in the den, in they come and settle on the rim of our glasses. A cheeky lot; they show up as if they'd been invited for cocktails. For some, their drinking habits are disastrous. At the end of happy hour, I will find a few dead flies floating around in my drink. For those unfortunate flies, one drink is too many, a thousand not enough. Many surviving fruit flies will continue to follow my breath even after I've finished my drink. Their appetites are insatiable.

Years ago, my offices were located in a large United Methodist church in Baltimore. In the fall, flies would begin appearing in the building, particularly around the window casings. They were not as big as horse flies, but larger than your average housefly. They looked overfed, plump and furry like woolly bears. The flies would appear religiously in early fall in our church offices so we called them Methodist flies. We meant no disrespect. We did not know what to make of them or what they should be properly called. We knew they were definitely not houseflies.

The Methodist flies manifested curious behaviors. They flew around slowly, languidly, not darting around frantically like other flies do as if the devil were chasing them. They savored time as though it was a precious commodity. The Methodist flies wandered slowly and sailed smoothly here and there around the rooms like gliders, as though curious and surveying their surroundings from the air. Some dropped gradually. Others abruptly took to the windowsills as if to gain a better view of the yard, while others reclined on their backs, buzzing quietly, contentedly, as if snoring as they napped. A couple seemed to just be sunning themselves. One staggered around as if drunk, although I dismissed the idea. The setting made it unlikely. Such a possibility would be more credible, say, in an Episcopal or Catholic church.

Living in the church, had the flies developed strong religious sensibilities? Had their faith led them to a more serene and reflective approach to the brevity of life and the immanence of death? Unlike fruit flies or horse flies that never seemed able to let go and relax, the Methodist flies appeared at peace with life and their maker, surrendering to what is, living in the present, not spending their days anxiously flitting from this to that, but living serenely with a sure and certain hope.

Soon after Hurricane Isabel hit Delmarva, flies appeared suddenly everywhere in my house, the same kind I'd seen in the Methodist church. I learned they are called cluster flies. In my home, I could just as well have called them Episcopal flies as Methodist, or if I were a Quaker, even Friends.

The horse flies' frenetic pursuit of cars never stopped until the air grew cooler and they disappeared as quickly as they'd appeared. I noticed, too, that in late fall, the fruit flies, having multiplied to frightful proportions, were suddenly gone overnight. Cluster flies, on the other hand, while slowed down considerably, lived well and as far as I could tell, happily into the winter.

I suspect that cluster flies, at least as I imagine them, have mastered the art of living. They live the measure of their days with an easy cadence, gently, still curious about their environment. They are not trying to be everywhere at once, like retirees who travel all the time and can't ever stay at home. At the end of the day, it's not longevity that's going to matter for any of us, anyway. What will matter is the quality of the time we have. And while, for all us critters, health is a significant factor in that quality of time, attitude also plays an important role. Cultivating a quiet spirit slows us down, the way deep breaths do, and helps us ride the ebb and flood of life gently as time passes us by.

Cardinal

CARDINAL VIRTUE

Cardinals live in the woods around our house. The males are small but stunning, especially in winter. I watch as they bounce in the snow like crimson balls. Unlike bluebirds, which are more resolute, sitting stoically with quiet dignity wherever they light, cardinals fidget, as if they were edgy, the way crooks behave before a heist—always looking shiftily over their shoulder. And, some cardinals are just plain nutty . . . or are they?

Not long ago, I noticed that the car's side-view mirrors were smudged, and that there were bird droppings on the door panels below. Not giving it much thought, I assumed that some weary bird made a temporary layover on my car, relieving himself before resuming his flight. In the coming weeks the droppings grew worse—the side panels of both our family cars were heavily littered with long white streaks of droppings. The side-view mirrors were so soiled that I could hardly see anything in them. What started as an anomaly became a regular occurrence.

At first I guessed the offenders were blackbirds. They're a nuisance—noisy and ugly birds and easy to blame. One day, however, out my study window I saw the culprit: a beautiful red cardinal, furiously assaulting my side-view mirror. He'd been heading for the same spot every day and carrying on shamelessly: This cardinal was obsessed with the side-view mirrors of our cars.

He was possessed. He flew at the mirror, again and again, fussing, pecking at it all over; he wouldn't stop. I called a friend of mine, a seasoned bird watcher, asking what she thought about his behavior: "Bonkers," she said. But I wondered if perhaps he was fiercely combative, with a pit bull's temperament, and, seeing his enemies in the mirror, was fighting them to the death. Or was he narcissistic, just another pretty face, and so enthralled with his own image that he lavished his likeness with abundant pecks and kisses? Whichever, he was fiercely determined.

We couldn't simply come home and just park anymore; every time we left the cars any length of time we had to cover their mirrors with plastic bags. If we didn't, the mirrors would be attacked . . . or ravished, as the case may be. I resented that so tiny a creature, by being so intrusive and making such a mess, could force a change in my lifestyle. I felt helpless, and outraged; I wanted to hit the cardinal with a rock.

Feeling so murderous offended my moral sensibilities. I began wondering, too, whether the cardinal's unnatural acts were a sign to me of my transgressions, in the way that the prophets' erratic behaviors were often considered divinely inspired rebukes. God instructed Ezekiel to eat a scroll to get sinners to pay heed to their wicked ways. Was this cardinal's nutty behavior also a sign? I recalled the biblical admonition, "He that is without sin among you, let him cast a stone." A hard saying for me in the heat of that moment as I watched the cardinal trashing the side-view mirrors of my car. Still, over the weeks, I grew less certain whether I was actually in the right, whether my wrath was justified. Was the cardinal intruding on my turf, or, by parking the car where I did, had I moved in on his space? When we share space with others, who is it that has the right to set the rules of behavior? Which of us could legitimately claim that the piece of land where I park my car was actually his?

I knew deep down that I didn't have a leg to stand on. As sure as God made little cardinals, wherever we settle down, we humans are the ones taking over everyone else's turf and then making a mess of it. Manhattan was an idyllic island when first purchased by the white man, with rivers filled with oysters, fish, and crabs, land thick with trees and filled with game, very much as the Eastern Shore once was. Now Manhattan is hardly fit to live in. All that's left there are pigeons, rats, roaches, and a few eagles with urban proclivities that like living on the parapets of the Cathedral of St. John the Divine and on top of high-end skyscrapers.

We eventually abandon these cities. Suburbs sprawl outward and we soon litter them and then flee to greener pastures where we fell more forests to build malls. We're left with density housing and formidable traffic. Where is a cardinal to go? It's no wonder no other critters want us around. The cardinal, by leaving his waste all over my car, may have been telling me just how he felt. Without so much as a peep, he had made an eloquent statement.

I know that we are an invasive species. I read recently that even as we reach for the stars, we've begun dumping tons of waste all over space, in heaven, right in God's front yard.

Since Sputnik's launch (according to *Harper's Index*), over 110,000 objects of less than half an inch are presently orbiting space. There are 8,870 objects larger than softballs, including 2,000 defunct satellites, hundreds of discarded rockets (about 6 explode every year), 34 nuclear-powered devices for space probes, and two burial satellites, one containing the ashes of Timothy Leary. It's become so littered that a concerned NASA is drafting "debris reduction" standards, including the establishment of a 21,650-mile-high "graveyard orbit" for those souls who may not trust God alone to admit them to heaven and then keep them there. There's no way that, if I were a cardinal, or an asteroid, for that matter, I would want one of my kind moving next door; it takes just one of us, and the whole neighborhood gets trashed.

About the cardinal? Whether his passions for a mirror are erotic, combative, or prophetic is anyone's guess. Whatever they are, he's still spending them regularly on my side-view mirrors. Is he "bonkers," as my friend has suggested? I think so, but again, who am I to say? I am a part of this insane consumerism that is now burying us alive in manufactured goods. Our will is being done in heaven as it is on earth.

Do I still want to kill the cardinal? I have no moral authority to cast the first stone. If God, in His mercy, hasn't yet whacked all of us, first for our thoughtless trespassing, trashing His creation, and then by adding insult to injury, leaving our garbage and dead bodies all over His front yard—military hardware to boot—the least I can do is to indulge the neurotic passions of one zany cardinal. The golden rule—do unto others—is a cardinal virtue; it's also the cornerstone of justice, whether the justice is environmental or social. Not sharing space respectfully with the rest of the world and the universe and then not cleaning up after ourselves is as bad for us as for the birds, in fact and is hardly a cardinal sin.

FLORA

Sunflowers

SUNFLOWERS

I inherited a melancholic disposition from my grandfather. I see it in the photographs of our family album. Our mouths incline downward at the edges, as if drawn by some unseen weight. Nature imparted to neither of us light hearts or happy faces.

I fight a moody tendency in two ways: by lecturing myself about my blessings—the way my mother used to prod me to finish everything on my plate by reminding me of the less fortunate people in India who had nothing to eat and how fortunate I was. The other way is by exercising. Lectures on my good fortune rarely work any personal changes—guilt provides poor incentives for a better attitude or for even doing good works—but exercise frequently helps both. Brisk walking mobilizes energy and afterward I'm more cheerful and positive. Walking is my exercise of choice.

During a heat wave some summers ago, walking became oppressive and I stopped my walks. But my mood grew darker for want of exercise. Then I decided to ride my bicycle between St. Michaels and Claiborne in the cool of early morning. The breeze that biking produces makes the heat more tolerable.

On Route 33, near the Bozman-Neavitt Road, I saw a field of sunflowers. I'd seen them before while driving in a car, but never did they seem as radiant as they looked that day from my bike. They were sirens beckoning me, wagging their heads seductively as I pedaled by, luring me closer, tempting me with their golden petals to abandon myself and tear recklessly across the road, traffic or not, just to be near them. One can't be too careful with sunflowers; they cast a spell.

At a break in traffic I walked my bike to the other side of the road by the field of sunflowers and entered the field. The sunflowers I'd first seen from the road were not the faces, but the backs of their heads. More than just another pretty face, sunflowers are as stunning from behind as they are head on, because by looking from behind their pedals lit by sun, they appear iridescent. The flowers were doing something no human being can do naturally, looking sunlight right in the eye. The sunflowers had no interest in me; their business was with the sun. These flowers not only bore a likeness to the sun. Sunflowers enjoy a mystical relationship to it.

Like the congregations of a church, the sunflowers stood in rows, dressed in their Sunday best. They were more like Quakers who worship silently than, say, Episcopalians, who, throughout a service, constantly pray, chatter, sing, or announce. And in the early morning breeze I watched as the sunflowers rocked their heads side to side, as if they were listening to the breeze or the sun delivering a homily, and each flower in an appreciative response, nodding gentle assent.

Walking among the rows of flowers, I caught myself tiptoeing—I felt a little silly, but now that I'd intruded into their happy solemnity, it seemed the least I could do was to be unobtrusive, even reverent. Discovering beauty inspires reverence.

Almost all of the sunflowers faced the sun in rapt attention, except in one corner of the field. There, by the shade of tall trees, a cluster of small sunflowers faced every which way, as if they were uncertain, not sure where to take their place, like parishioners who come late to a service and not sure where to sit. Some held their heads high, confidently, almost defiantly. Others with bent necks dropped their heads low, as if they were ashamed. No two of the sunflowers faced the same way. I wondered why. Then I saw that the shade from the tall trees fell in this corner of the field. As the sun rose, exposing the sunflowers to the light, I suspected they were caught looking the wrong way and were now, in a manner of speaking, getting their heads on straight.

In time it became murderously hot and I was sweating profusely. Flies began breakfasting on me. Although uncomfortable, I felt something rising up deep inside me like a hiccup—it wasn't indigestion, but pure, spontaneous delight. I wanted to giggle and then laugh out loud. I was surprised by joy, and the pleasure that comes with being surrounded by sunflowers' cheery faces as they commune with the sun. Although I was the stranger among these creatures with whom I shared space on this day, they extended to me the ancient law of hospitality, welcoming me into their midst. They simply offered me their delight, lots of it. And while I pedaled on home, I knew that the ends of my mouth which normally incline downward, were turned up, toward the sun, and for a while, whenever I thought about the sunflowers, I'd smile.

Requiem

REQUIEM FOR A SUNFLOWER

Just the other day I walked by the field of sunflowers on Route 33, the ones that I'd seen only a few weeks ago. They were beautiful then, but now, instead of radiant yellow heads held high, the sunflowers looked as if they'd been stricken by plague. Heads were bent low, half over their stalks, and their faces, once pulsating energy, had now darkened and looked weary. Their petals had been thick and luxuriant, but now they hung thin and scraggly. I was troubled by what I saw and sat down next to the sunflowers, wondering about this startling change, hoping what I saw might teach me wisdom about life, about aging, and about death. Why not sunflowers? We've considered the lilies of the field for centuries.

Over me, cumulus clouds billowed upward like incense into the blue sky and the sun beat down relentlessly on the back of the sunflower's heads. The grass I sat on was dry and crunchy but provided me with nature's own mat on which to sit as I contemplated the meaning of this sad sight. The moment seemed divinely inspired and a romantic feeling pervaded the moment as if I were seated momentarily at the still point of the universe, or like the Buddha about to be enlightened.

I was wearing shorts. Ants had begun making their way up my leg. A few made it successfully underneath the shorts and soon there were ants in my pants. Meditation became difficult. It's hard to concentrate, especially as there were three ants and each one had to be chased down, or more accurately, up, in order to be expunged. I stood up to get at the ants and sat down after the all clear.

I got rid of the ants but could think of little else; each tiny sensation on my legs might prove to be more ants. What I hoped would be a moment of truth soon fell apart, at least the moment as I tried to contrive it, and I finally bagged my attempt to meditate on the meaning of life in favor of avoiding the ants.

The formal art of meditation, which has been around at least three thousand years, attempts to help us accept what in life we cannot change, encouraging us to be gently present to how things are. Sound simple? Not for me. I always seem to have an agenda. But how was it for me, in those moments by the dying sunflowers? Simply put, I was very sad that the sunflowers were dying; I felt a pain of loss in my heart as I recalled how lovely they had been, how much pleasure they'd afforded me only a few weeks before, and in the middle of all those tender sentiments, I struggled to fetch ants from my pants.

Maybe truth was there all the time, right under my nose, or, more precisely, creeping up my leg: What's often most challenging in the meanest or the most sublime moments of our lives is how we manage the bugs that always attend those moments. At first I thought that the ants were an intrusion, keeping my soul from its nobler tasks. I don't think so now. Entomologists know that whatever we humans are about, good or bad, for sure it's going to be full of bugs. I think wisdom is the art of dealing as best we can with the bugs that beset us.

As I stood, ready to take my leave, I began noticing bugs everywhere; ants marched up and down the stalks of the flowers, several wasps made their way lazily among the flowers along with numerous flies and yellow bees. The bugs weren't intruders, but as nature would have it, significant players in the lives of each of these flowers from the time their tiny shoots first broke ground. The story of the sunflower is also the story of insects; they're all mixed up together; in life, everything is connected. In fact, it will probably be bugs that will remain with the sunflowers long after everyone has left them to their fate.

I've noticed at funerals that it's not when the preacher eulogizes the deceased that my heart feels touched—preachers make the deceased bigger than life—but afterward, in the small talk, when we hear about the "bugs" in the life of the deceased, those goofy stories, like how Aunt Alice left the wedding invitations on top of the car to get her keys, forgot they were there and drove away, covering the countryside with colorful invitations to a wedding. We're probably loved more for our bugs than our virtues, and since there are always more bugs, it's a good thing. God, thank heaven, is accepting of both.

I'm thankful for the short lives of these sunflowers on Route 33. Their youthful beauty brought delight to my heart, and by their dying, a measure of humility. I can't be as God, understanding the meaning of life and death, but I can try to work out the bugs that appear in my life, one at a time, as best I can, and live as gracefully as possible with those I can't.

SAILING INTO
THE SUNSET

Periplus

PERIPLUS

Periplus is a Greek word. It's also the name I gave our sailboat, a 38-foot cutter. In Greek, the word means "sailing around." For twenty-eight years we sailed around the Bay aboard *Periplus*. The word also refers to an ancient Greek naval strategy, how a flotilla encircles its enemy's ships before launching an attack.

Periplus generated stories about the Bay and about us that have lasted long after she was gone.

One day we went out for a sail. The wind blew briskly. It would drop occasionally, but in a few minutes return with gusto. Finally the air became still and we were becalmed.

Legions of Japanese beetles set upon us; they surrounded our sailboat, as though they had formed a *periplus* and were attacking us from all quarters. We were defenseless. Everything aboard, including sails, cordage, compass, our flotation cushions, and the white fiberglass deck was stained with a greenish deposit each beetle left behind on whatever it struck before the beetle was either killed or withdrew. The beetles got in our hair. The assault lasted about an hour. It ended. This was only one adventure aboard *Periplus*, a boat that was a part of our lives. It was a source of delight, a way of being together while discovering the strange and glorious ways of the Bay of the Mother of God.

Life is about good times and bad: the threads from each weave what comprises the whole fabric of our lives.

Where I live, in Talbot County on the Eastern Shore, the median age is about forty-seven and a half. A significant number living here are retirees who arrived from other places. Many came to spend their latter years in a rural environment with access to boating. Sailing is especially popular, and many bumper stickers on cars I see announce to the driver following them that "I'd rather be sailing."

Growing older is an experience hard to communicate to someone who has not begun feeling its nuances. It's not aches and pains so much, at first, but the subtle shifts in attitudes and inclinations. I thought at first as if the world was changing. The world was indeed changing, but I know now that what I was feeling was not a changing world, but an aging me. Aging, like breathing, I do all the time, have no control over it and am hardly aware that it's happening except when the breathing feels different from what I'm accustomed to. I think a lot more about breathing then.

I've noticed for myself and among my contemporaries who are sailors that giving up the boat is a decision made with mixed feelings, experienced as a significant milestone in one's life. There is sadness, as if when we decide to get rid of the boat, a large part of our story is over and will go with her. The expense, energy, and care that a boat like ours required,—outfitting her in the spring, hauling her out in the fall, routine maintenance (all of which were once welcomed as part of the adventure)—now seemed burdensome.

Picking *Periplus* up from Oxford Boat Yard after her winter hiatus had become a rite of passage for us over the years. Leaving the yard and breaking out onto the open water, after a long confining winter had ended, was exhilarating. I always felt infinite satisfaction bringing her to homeport and seeing her rocking at the dock as though she was pleased to be home. On those spring days when we sailed her home, the sun would typically be warm while the air remained chilly. The smell of water—not salt, but fresh—filled and cleansed my nostrils and lungs. I breathed more easily.

I was never a bold sailor. In fact I told friends that I was "chicken of the sea," never venturing out in foul weather and scurrying for shelter before four in the afternoon to duck the summer squalls that the Bay of the Mother of God, named ironically after the gentle saint, incongruously fomented. I'd been sailing since I was sixteen—but I was more of a romantic about being on the water than an adventurer, as if sailing was about chasing dreams, attempts at reassembling the scattered images of my early days growing up on an island where water was everywhere. I'd almost catch the dream, but never quite. I couldn't wait to try again on the next cruise. That much about sailing was very personal to me alone.

My wife began losing interest in sailing some years before I did. The change came more quickly for her. When living on the Western Shore, sailing was our escape. After we retired and moved to St. Michaels on the Eastern Shore, she felt that by being here she had already escaped, so there was no need any more to "get away." We continued to cruise and she participated because it was time for us to spend together, which she valued, but not a way of being together in the way that she once liked. Her energies were gravitating to carpentry and art and mine were spent learning to write and making black-and-white photographs as I had done since I was a boy.

A couple of years before we put *Periplus* up for adoption I accepted the fact that my wife was less interested, so I decided to practice sailing solo. A 38-foot cutter is not easy to manage, but I practiced and did well and installed a mooring off the waterfront so I could spare myself the complexities of docking alone (which in heavy wind can be hazardous). I was free to come and go at will without a crew. I enjoyed the freedom to come and go without depending on someone else to join me, and I sailed now on impulse rather than by consultation and planning.

I'm glad I made the decision to learn to solo *Periplus*. In taking those short excursions around the Choptank, it was as if I had come full circle and was recapitulating the first joy of sailing a boat that I had experienced as a boy.

Growing up, my sister had a small Penguin class sailboat. She let me sail it. We lived on Staten Island and I sailed out of Great Kills harbor. Carrying the sails in a duffel bag, I'd take the bus from home—sails then were cotton and needed to be kept dry at home—and in the latter part of the day take the boat out for a sail by myself.

I'd sail up toward the Narrows, keeping several yards from the beach, which gave me the illusion of greater speed than I was actually traveling. I sailed near where the early explorer Verrazano anchored his ship, the *Dolphin*, in 1524, and first saw Staten Island from the water. Earlier in the same year he had also sailed into the Chesapeake Bay and called it Arcadia, the name suggesting that he'd come upon an unspoiled wilderness.

I'd listen to the chatter the water made slapping the plywood hull as she sped along and I watched the commercial shipping leaving and entering New York Harbor. I was alone, but I did not feel lonely. I experienced what I now understand is solitude, that way of being by oneself and knowing that I am in tune with the world. Those brief excursions filled me with longing, a kind of hunger, but I could think of no food that would have sated the desire. It's not an unpleasant sensation, more an anticipation of something waiting for me, as if I am yards ahead of myself, like a shadow that is cast before me that I have yet to catch up to, a shadow created from a light somewhere behind me.

In several day sails I made alone on the Choptank River with *Periplus*, I relived those days of boyhood discovery and once, while heading out from the mouth of Broad Creek into the Choptank, that hunger arose again and I felt the joy that often comes with heightened awareness, the way mystics speak about how eternity is right there in the moment. The mystic Julian of Norwich once wrote that once she beheld a hazelnut in her palm and wondered about what it was that she saw. Through "the eyes of my understanding" she wrote, she understood that what she was seeing was "all that is made." It's through the eyes of our understanding that we may see an eternity in the grain of sand or perhaps see it in a sailboat at the remains of the day. Moments like that are not contrived, they just happen.

It was time to sell Periplus. We had her on the market for over a year. It's the way of aging that the old lose value in the world's marketplace or worse still, nobody thinks your worth having. We'd dropped the price but still no bites. We decided it might be a dignified end to our time together with Periplus to give her the Chesapeake Bay Maritime Museum to sell at auction. In that community, we felt that Periplus was sure to find a home where she could be loved and cared for. The tax break would offer some financial compensation but the loss was ultimately not financial, it was the loss of the visible signs a mutual history.

With two dear friends we took her on the last sail from Broad Creek up around Tilghman Island and left her at the Maritime Museum. It was a glorious sail except for the nagging feeling that this was the end of an era. Indeed it was.

We popped open a bottle of Champagne, toasted her and left her at the Museum's pier where we docked her. As we left, I couldn't look back. I felt like I had some years ago when we had to put down our dog Spunky. Doing the right thing doesn't always feel right.

She's gone. And with her the outward and visible sign of all kinds of inner graces I discovered aboard *Periplus*—including a few violent storms and inhospitable beetles.

For me, the end of the sailing journey became a time for turning more inward, to digest the adventures that sailing brought to my wife and me. It has become a time to cull from the stories those pieces that point beyond themselves to the meaning of what a life is about. And life is, at the end of our days, all about discovery. I'm glad I have had many of my discoveries aboard *Periplus* on the Bay of the Mother of God.